Honoring Mary with the Holy Father

Compiled and edited by
Jaymie Stuart Wolfe

With an Introduction by
Marianne Lorraine Trouvé, FSP

Pauline
BOOKS & MEDIA
Boston

Nihil Obstat: Reverend Robert W. Oliver, S.T.D., J.C.D.

Imprimatur: ✠ Seán P. Cardinal O'Malley, O.F.M., Cap.
　　　　　　Archbishop of Boston
　　　　　　May 18, 2011

Library of Congress Cataloging-in-Publication Data

Honoring Mary with the Holy Father / compiled and edited by Jaymie Stuart Wolfe; with an introduction by Marianne Lorraine Trouvé.
　　p. cm. -- (Thoughts and prayers of the popes for young Catholics)
　　ISBN 0-8198-3409-2 (pbk.)
　　1. Mary, Blessed Virgin, Saint--Prayers and devotions. 2. Catholic children--Prayers and devotions. I. Wolfe, Jaymie Stuart. II. Title. III. Series.
　　BX2160.23.H66 2011
　　242'.74--dc23

2011017991

Published by Pauline Books & Media, 50 Saint Pauls Avenue, Boston, MA 02130-3491

Printed in U.S.A.
HMHF VSAUSAPEOILL6-1J11-03700 3409-2

www.pauline.org

Pauline Books & Media is the publishing house of the Daughters of St. Paul, an international congregation of women religious serving the Church with the communications media.

1 2 3 4 5 6 7 8 9　　　　　　　　　　　　　　　　15 14 13 12 11

Thoughts and Prayers of the Popes for
Young Catholics

Praying with the Holy Father

Honoring Mary with the Holy Father

Adoring Jesus with the Holy Father

Table of Contents

Introduction

Two thousand years ago, God sent an angel named Gabriel to a young, Jewish woman named Mary. Gabriel said to her, "God has a special plan for you! He wants you to be the mother of Jesus, his Son. Will you accept?" Because Mary always wanted to do whatever God asked, she immediately answered, "Yes! I will! Let it happen to me as you have said!" From that day on, the history of the world changed.

After the angel came, the first thing Mary did was to go visit her cousin Elizabeth. Elizabeth too was expecting a baby, who would be John the Baptist. When the two of them met, Mary praised God. The Gospel of Luke records her song of praise. In it, Mary said, "All generations will call me blessed, for God has done great things for me!"

So here we are over two thousand years later, still honoring Mary, just as she said in her *Magnificat* of praise. But when we honor Mary, we are really honoring God. From all the women who ever lived in every place and time, Mary was God's choice. Like Mary, we praise and thank God. We call her blessed because through her, God gave the world the greatest gift of all: Jesus Christ. Mary doesn't seek honor for herself. She wants to bring us to Jesus.

When Jesus grew up, he left home and began to preach the Good News. He attracted people who followed him. Jesus chose twelve of them to be his apostles, and he made Peter the leader of the group. After Jesus died, rose from the dead, and went to heaven, Peter went to Rome and became head of the Church there. When he died, Peter's role as leader passed on to others who took his place. So all through the centuries there has been one pope after another to lead the Church and teach us about Jesus.

The popes have also taught us about Mary, and left us many thoughts and prayers in her honor. This book brings together some of the most beautiful of these prayers and reflections. You can pray them, too.

Don't just read through this book as you would any other book. Take one page or section at a time, and pray with the Holy Father who wrote the words on that page. Make him a part of your prayer time, and become part of his prayer time, too! If that sounds impossible, remember that prayer places us all in God's presence. So, through prayer, we can be together even with people who lived hundreds of years before we were born!

A lot of what the popes have to tell us is interesting and inspiring. But the words popes use can be hard to understand. Sometimes the vocabulary is formal or unfamiliar. Sometimes the meaning of what a pope says is challenging. That is why we have made this book. With the approval of *Libreria Editrice Vaticana*, *Honoring Mary with the Holy Father* gives you the prayers and words of the popes in bite–sized pieces, and in language that is easier to pray and understand.

The thoughts and prayers in these pages come from many different times. They were written by popes who were quite different from each other. At the end of this book is a section of very short biographies, so that you can learn something about the popes you have prayed with.

So, find a place to be with God, and invite a pope to come along. After all, the Holy Fathers—if they could—would certainly take time to honor Mary with you.

—*Sister Marianne Lorraine Trouvé, Daughters of St. Paul*

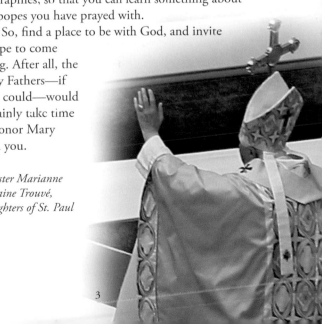

Servant of the Lord

a woman who loves

Mary
of Nazareth

show us Jesus

lead us to him

teach us to know him

and to love him

Among the saints, Mary is outstanding. She is the Mother of the Lord and the mirror of all holiness. Mary's greatness lies in the fact that she wants to bring glory to God, not to herself. She is humble: her only desire is to be the servant of the Lord (cf. Lk 1:38, 48). Mary knows that she will contribute to the salvation of the world, but only if she serves God's plans completely, instead of carrying out her own projects.

—BENEDICT XVI
Deus Caritas Est, 41
December 25, 2005

*H*ail Mary, humble servant of the Lord,
and glorious Mother of Jesus Christ!
O faithful, holy Virgin Mary,
the Word of God found a home in you.
Teach us how to keep listening to the Word,
and respond to the voice of the Holy Spirit.
Show us how to hear his call in our deepest
     thoughts,
and see his presence in the events of history.

—JOHN PAUL II
Prayer to Our Lady of Lourdes
August 15, 2004

Mary is at home with the Word of God. She moves in and out of it with ease. She speaks and thinks with the Word of God. The Word of God becomes her word. Mary's thoughts are in tune with God's, and her will is one with his.

. . . Mary is a woman who loves. How could it be otherwise? As a faithful believer who thinks with God's thoughts and wills with God's will, she cannot fail to be a woman who loves.

—BENEDICT XVI
Deus Caritas Est, 41
December 25, 2005

Adam found hope in Mary crushing the serpent's head, and dried the tears that sin had brought to his eyes.

Noah envisioned Mary when he was shut safely into the ark.
Abraham imagined her when he was prevented from sacrificing his son.

Jacob, when he dreamt of the ladder on which angels ascended and descended;
Moses, when he was amazed by the flaming bush that did not burn;
David, when he brought the Ark of the Covenant into Jerusalem with dancing and singing;
Elijah, when he saw the distant rain cloud rise out of the sea:

All these encounters point to Mary, because through her, all of God's promises are fulfilled.

—Pius X
Ad Diem Illum Laetissimum, 6
February 2, 1904

Mary shows us what love is and where it comes from, as well as how its power is constantly renewed.

We place the Church and our mission of love into her hands.

Holy Mary, Mother of God,
you have given the world its true light,
    Jesus.
You gave yourself completely to God's call,
and this became a spring of the goodness
    that flows from him.
Show us Jesus. Lead us to him.
Teach us to know him and to love him,
so that we can become capable of true love
and be fountains of living water in a thirsty
    world.

—BENEDICT XVI
Deus Caritas Est, 42
December 25, 2005

Women today will be pleasantly surprised to see that even though she served God completely, Mary of Nazareth was far from being a fearful, weak woman. Instead, Mary did not hesitate to proclaim that God defends the humble and victims of injustice, and that God removes the powerful people of this world from their positions (cf. Lk 1:51–53). Women of today will see Mary . . . as a woman of strength, who experienced poverty and suffering, escape and exile (cf. Mt 2: 13–23).

—PAUL VI
Marialis Cultus, 37
February 2, 1974

Hail, Star of the Sea!

Role Model

life is like a voyage
in which we watch
for the stars
that will show us
the route

O Immaculate Mother, . . . your beauty shows us that the victory of love is possible, that it is certain. Your beauty shows us that grace is stronger than sin. . . .

Mary, help us to trust even more in what is good. Teach us to count on giving freely, on service, on non-violence, and on the power of the truth. Encourage us to stay alert, not to give into the temptation of easy escapes. Give us the strength to face reality and its problems with courage and responsibility. This is what you did when, as a young woman, you were called to stake everything on the Word of the Lord.

—BENEDICT XVI
Homage to the Immaculate at the Spanish Steps
December 8, 2008

Christians should follow the example of the most holy Virgin Mary because Jesus himself gave her to us as our Mother. He has pointed to her as the model we should follow. It is, in fact, a natural thing that children should have hearts like their mothers and should reflect their mothers' goodness and virtues.

—PAUL VI
Signum Magnum, 5
May 13, 1967

And so we hope that those who reflect on the example Mary offers us, may be more and more convinced of the value of a human life given completely to carrying out the heavenly Father's will and to bringing good to others.

—PIUS XII
Munificentissimus Deus, 42
1950

Everything about Mary leads us to her Son. His excellence made her immaculate and full of grace. Everything about Mary inspires us to praise the Holy Trinity. So it was that Bernadette, while praying her Rosary at the cave, learned how she should give glory to God—Father, Son, and Holy Spirit—from the words and presence of the Blessed Virgin.

—PIUS XII
Le Pelerinage de Lourdes, 23
July 2, 1957

First, the Church has always pointed to the Virgin Mary as an example for us. We should imitate Mary, but not the type of life she led or the world in which she lived. Mary is held up as a role model because she fully accepted the will of God. She heard the word of God and acted on it. Charity and a spirit of service were the driving forces of her actions. Mary is worth following because she was the first and most perfect of Christ's disciples.

—PAUL VI
Marialis Cultus, 35
February 2, 1974

In a hymn written more than a thousand years ago, the Church has greeted Mary, the Mother of God, singing,
"*Ave, maris stella*!" "Hail, star of the sea!"

Human life is a journey; but toward what destination?
How do we find the way?

Life is like a voyage on the sea of history, often dark and stormy, a voyage in which we watch for the stars that will show us the route.

—BENEDICT XVI
Spe Salvi, 49
November 30, 2007

The true stars of our life are the people who have lived good lives. They are lights of hope. Certainly, Jesus Christ is the true light, the sun that has risen above all the shadows of history. But to reach him we also need lights close by—people who shine with his light and so guide us along our way. Who more than Mary could be a star of hope for us?

—BENEDICT XVI
Spe Salvi, 49
November 30, 2007

Blessed
Mother

when I was a child
I learned to love you
as a mother,
turn to you in danger,
and trust in your prayers

From the very beginning, even before time began, the eternal Father chose and prepared a mother for his only-begotten Son.

God loved Mary above all other creatures, and in her the Father was especially pleased and delighted. Therefore, God poured out to her even more heavenly treasures than he has given to all the angels and saints. . . . Under God, we cannot even imagine anything greater. Outside of God, none of us can understand it fully.

—Pius IX
Ineffabilis Deus
December 8, 1854

O Mary,
since I was a baby, your name has been on
    my lips
and in my heart.

When I was a child
I learned to love you as a mother,
turn to you in danger,
and trust in your prayers.

You see in my heart the desire to know the
    truth,
to practice virtue,
to be wise and just,
strong and patient,
and a brother to all.

—Attributed to John XXIII

$\mathcal{M}$ary, you are the Mother of the human family and of the nations.
We place all humanity into your hands,
with its hopes and fears.

Give us the light of true wisdom.
Guide our steps in the ways of peace.
Enable all people to meet Christ, the Way,
the Truth, and the Life.

Support us, O Virgin Mary, on our journey
    of faith,
and gain for us the grace of eternal salvation.
O merciful, O loving, O sweet Mother of
    God,
and our Mother, Mary!

—JOHN PAUL II
Prayer to Our Lady of the Millennium

How right and natural it is when Christian souls turn to Mary for help! They confidently share with her their future hopes and past achievements, their sorrows and joys. They place themselves like children in the care of a generous mother.

—Leo XIII
Adiutricem, 8
September 5, 1895

When we turn to Mary in prayer, we turn to the Mother of Mercy. She loves us so much, that whatever we need, especially to reach eternal life, she comes instantly to our sides, even when we have not called on her.

—Leo XIII
Magnae Dei Matris, 9
September 8, 1892

O Mary,
help the church of Christ
to recognize you as our Mother, Daughter,
    and Sister;
the best example for us;
and our glory, joy, and hope.

We ask you to show each of us how to
    honor you
because of who you are and what you do
in God's amazing and loving plan of
    salvation.

O Holy Virgin, help us praise you!

—PAUL VI
You Are Our Mother

O Mary,
hear the cry which rises up from every heart.
Tenderly bend over our painful wounds.
Convert those who do evil,
dry the tears of those who are troubled or
    helpless,
comfort all who are poor and humble.
Blessed Mother,
quench hate, sweeten harshness,
guard the flower of purity in the young,
protect the holy Church,
draw all people to Christian goodness.

O sweetest Mother, receive our humble
    prayers.
But more than anything else,
bring us to that day of happiness with you,
when we may sing at your throne in heaven
the hymn we sing today around your altars
    on earth.

Amen.

—Pius XII
Prayer in Honor of the 100th Anniversary of the
Dogma of the Immaculate Conception, 1954

like you at Bethlehem's crib

and at Calvary's cross,

I want to stay close to Jesus always

Help of Christians

make us aware of our

vocation and our mission

may we not be unworthy

to represent Christ

O Mary,
help me live as a faithful disciple of Jesus,
to build up Christian society,
and bring joy to the holy Catholic Church.

I greet you, Mother, morning and evening.
I pray to you as I go on my way.
I hope for the inspiration and
encouragement from you
that will help me
to keep the holy promises of my vocation on
    earth,
to give glory to God,
and to gain eternal salvation.

O Mary!
Like you at Bethlehem's crib and at Calvary's
    cross,
I want to stay close to Jesus always.
He is the eternal King of all ages and all
peoples.
Amen.

—ATTRIBUTED TO JOHN XXIII

The mightiest helper of the Christian people, and the most merciful, is the Virgin Mother of God. How right it is to honor Mary more and more, and to call upon her for help with confidence that grows every day. The many blessings of all kinds flowing from Mary over the whole world are gifts for all people. They constantly add new reasons to call on her and honor her.

—LEO XIII
Adiutricem, 1
September 5, 1895

In times of public disaster and personal need, Christians of every era turn to Mary, asking that she come to their aid and relieve the suffering of their bodies and souls. Those who sought Mary's help with faithful and trusting prayer have never hoped in vain.

—Pius XI
Ingravescentibus Malis, 3
September 29, 1937

$\mathcal{M}$ary, make us aware of our vocation and
our mission.
May we not be unworthy to represent
Christ and be his presence
in our priesthood,
in our words,
and in giving our lives for the faithful
people
he has placed in our hands.

O you who are full of grace,
may the priesthood that honors you,
also be holy and immaculate.

Amen.

—Paul VI
You Are Our Mother

O Virgin Mary, lovely as the moon,
joy of the angels and saints in heaven,
help us to become like you.
Give our souls a ray of your beauty
which does not fade with the years
but shines into eternity.

O Mary, sun of heaven,
bring life where there is death
and enlighten spirits where there is darkness.
Turn your face toward your children,
and shine your light and warmth on us.

—Pius XII
Mary Our Strength

O Mary, powerful as an army,
give victory to us.
We are very weak, and our enemy rages with
pride.
But under your banner we believe we can
overcome him.

Save us, O Mary,
lovely as the moon,
bright as the sun,
awesome as an army ready for battle,
and fed not by hatred, but by the fire of
love.
Amen.

—Pius XII
Mary Our Strength

Prayers of the Rosary

Apostles' Creed

I believe in God,
the Father almighty,
Creator of heaven and earth,
and in Jesus Christ, his only Son, our Lord,
who was conceived by the Holy Spirit,
born of the Virgin Mary,
suffered under Pontius Pilate,
was crucified, died, and was buried;
he descended into hell;
on the third day he rose again from the dead;
he ascended into heaven,
and is seated at the right hand of God
    the Father almighty;
from there he will come to judge the living
    and the dead.

I believe in the Holy Spirit,
the holy catholic Church,
the communion of saints,
the forgiveness of sins,
the resurrection of the body,
and life everlasting. Amen.

Hail Mary

Hail Mary, full of grace, the Lord is with you. Blessed are you among women, and blessed is the fruit of your womb, Jesus. Holy Mary, Mother of God, pray for us sinners, now and at the hour of our death. Amen.

Our Father

Our Father, who art in heaven, hallowed be thy name. Thy kingdom come, thy will be done on earth as it is in heaven. Give us this day our daily bread, and forgive us our trespasses, as we forgive those who trespass against us. And lead us not into temptation, but deliver us from evil. Amen.

Glory

Glory be to the Father, and to the Son, and to the Holy Spirit: as it was in the beginning, is now, and will be for ever. Amen.

Fatima or Decade Prayer

O my Jesus, forgive us our sins, save us from the fires of hell. Lead all souls to heaven, especially those most in need of your mercy.

Hail, Holy Queen

Hail, holy Queen, Mother of mercy, our life, our sweetness, and our hope. To you do we cry, poor banished children of Eve; to you do we send up our sighs mourning and weeping in this valley of tears. Turn then, most gracious advocate, your eyes of mercy toward us; and after this our exile, show unto us the blessed fruit of your womb, Jesus. O clement, O loving, O sweet Virgin Mary.

Joyful Mysteries

The Annunciation
The Visitation
The Nativity
The Presentation in the Temple
Finding of Jesus in the Temple

Luminous Mysteries

The Baptism of Jesus
The Wedding at Cana
Jesus Announces God's Kingdom
The Transfiguration
Jesus Gives Us the Holy Eucharist

Sorrowful Mysteries

The Agony in the Garden
The Scourging at the Pillar
The Crowning with Thorns
The Carrying of the Cross
The Crucifixion

Glorious Mysteries

The Resurrection
The Ascension
The Descent of the Holy Spirit
The Assumption of Mary
The Coronation of Mary

The Rosary

by praying
the Rosary,
those in heaven
and on earth
share their feelings,
words and actions

To pray the Rosary we use a set of beads. At the surface, the beads help us count "Hail Marys." But they can also be symbolic of something deeper.

Notice first that the beads join at the Crucifix, which both opens and closes the prayer. Likewise, our whole life and prayer center on Christ. Everything begins in him, and leads to him.

. . . Counting the beads to mark our progress is like the unending path of Christian prayer and perfection. We can also let the beads remind us of our many relationships and the communion and friendship which unites us all in Christ.

—JOHN PAUL II
Rosarium Virginis Mariae, 36
October 16, 2002

Families come together infrequently, and when they do, they are often taken up with watching television. A return to praying the Rosary as a family means filling your daily life with very different images, images of our salvation.

A family that prays the Rosary together becomes something like the Holy Family's household in Nazareth. Its members place Jesus at the center, share his joys and sorrows, place their needs in his hands, and draw the hope and the strength to go on, from him.

. . . Why not try it?

—JOHN PAUL II,
Rosarium Virginis Mariae, 41, 42
October 16, 2002

O Mary, you are praying for us,
you are always praying for us.
We know it, and we feel it.
Oh what joy and truth, and what
magnificent glory
the Rosary always brings us!
By praying the Rosary, those in heaven and
on earth share their feelings, words, and
    actions.
Praying the Rosary soothes our human
    troubles;
it gives us a taste of the peace that does not
    belong to this world,
and the hope of eternal life!

—Attributed to John XXIII

The pleasant memories of my younger
days have not faded or vanished as the years
have passed. On the contrary . . . my many
years have made Mary's Rosary even dearer
to me. I never fail to recite it each day. . . .

—JOHN XXIII
Grata Recordatio, 3
September 26, 1959

44

$\mathcal{I}$ do not hesitate to say publicly that I have great confidence in the Holy Rosary for healing the evils of our times, not with force, not with weapons, not with human power, but with God's help received through this prayer. The Church is strong like David with his sling, and able to face the enemy with the words David spoke as a young shepherd:

"You come to me with sword, and spear, and javelin; but I come to you in the name of the Lord of Hosts . . . the battle is the Lord's, and he will give you into our hand" (1 Sam 17:45a, 47b).

—PIUS XII
Ingruentium Malorum, 15
September 15, 1951

There are three things which seem to be pulling society down. First, distaste for a simple and hard-working life; second, the desire to avoid suffering of any kind; third, forgetfulness of the life to come. Let us seek a cure for these evils in the Rosary. . . . For I am convinced that if it is prayed from the heart, the Rosary will benefit not only the person who prays it, but all of society.

—Leo XIII
Laetitiae Sanctae, 3, 4, 6
September 8, 1893

Against the background of the words "Hail Mary," the main events of Jesus's life pass before the eyes of the soul. These events take shape in the joyful, sorrowful, and glorious mysteries. They put us in touch with Jesus through the heart of his Mother, Mary.

In the decades of the Rosary, our hearts can also embrace all the events that make up the lives of people, families, nations, the Church, and all humankind. This includes our needs and the needs of our neighbors, those who are closest to us. In this way the simple prayer of the Rosary marks the rhythm of human life.

—JOHN PAUL II
Rosarium Virginis Mariae, 2
October 16, 2002

help all who are in trouble,

give courage to those who are weak,

comfort those who are sad,

heal those who are sick

Pray for Us

*H*oly Immaculate Mary,
help all who are in trouble.
Give courage to those who are weak,
comfort those who are sad,
heal those who are sick.
O Mary, pray for the people,
speak for the clergy,
give special care to nuns.

Holy Mary, may all feel and enjoy your kind
and powerful help.
May all who honor you now, and will
always honor you,
offer you their requests.

Hear all our prayers, O Mother,
and answer them all.
We are all your children:
answer the prayers of your children.

Amen forever.

—JOHN XXIII
Prayer of Love for Mary

O Immaculate Virgin, I give you all the "little ones" of our city: first, the children, especially those who are seriously ill, disabled, or suffer difficult family situations. Watch over them and help them feel the warmth of God's love in the care of those who are beside them!

To you, O Mary, I give those who are lonely, elderly, sick; immigrants finding it hard to adjust, families finding it difficult to make ends meet, and people who cannot find a job or who have lost a job. Teach us, Mary, to show unity with those who struggle, and to fill the social gaps that grow between us.

—BENEDICT XVI
Homage to the Immaculate at the Spanish Steps
December 8, 2008

The part which the Virgin Mary played and still plays in the progress, battles, and victories of the Catholic faith shows us what God has planned for her to do. It should fill the hearts of all good people with hope to gain those things which we all desire. Trust Mary, and ask her aid.

—Leo XIII
Adiutricem, 15
September 5, 1895

O Mary,
look upon all people,
and on this world in which God's will calls
us to live and work today.

Our world has turned its back on the light
of Christ,
but then fears and cries out against the
frightening shadows that it has created.

O most beautiful Virgin, most worthy
Mother,
may your voice invite the world to turn its
eyes to the life that is the light of all.
O blessed among women, may the world
turn toward you, the first lamp of Christ,
who is the only and highest light of world.

—PAUL VI
You Are Our Mother

$\mathcal{M}$ost holy Virgin,
 . . . in your body and soul,
in your faith and love,
 . . . look kindly on us as we ask for your
      powerful protection.
The evil serpent, upon whom the first curse
      was laid,
continues to attack and tempt the children
      of Eve.

Blessed Mother, our Queen and Helper,
you crushed the enemy's head at the first
moment of your conception.
We ask you to gather our prayers together
and present them before God's throne.

May we never be caught in the traps laid
      for us,
but reach the gates of salvation.

May the Church and Christian society
      once more
sing the song of deliverance, of victory, and
      of peace.
Amen.

—Pius X
Prayer in Honor of the 50th Anniversary of the
Dogma of the Immaculate Conception, 1903

$\mathcal{M}$ost Blessed Virgin, look on all your children with a mother's mercy. Consider the worry of bishops who fear that their flocks will suffer a terrible storm of evils. Listen to the pain of so many people, fathers and mothers of families uncertain about their future and burdened by hardships and cares. Soothe the minds of those at war and inspire them with "thoughts of peace." Through your prayers, may God be merciful. May he give peace to the nations that seek it, and bring them to a lasting age of true riches.

—Paul VI
Christ Matri, 13
September 15, 1966

Mary rules over the whole world
with a mother's goodness
even though she is crowned
in heaven with
the glory of a queen

may Mary's most tender love
be moved to gain the peace
we seek for our troubled world

Queen
of Heaven

O Mother of Faith,
you went to the Temple with Jesus,
the one God promised to Abraham, Isaac,
    Jacob,
and all the fathers.

Mary, Ark of the Covenant,
give glory to God the Father,
and bring him now the priests of your Son.

O Mother of the Church,
among the disciples in the Upper Room you
    prayed to the Holy Spirit
for the new people of God and their
    shepherds.

O Queen of the Apostles,
gain for all priests a full measure of gifts.

—JOHN PAUL II
Pastores Dabo Vobis, 82
March 25, 1992

God asked Mary, a humble young woman
of Nazareth, to become the Mother of
the Messiah. Mary answered this request
with a gift of her whole self, and joined
her unconditional "yes" to that of her Son,
Jesus. She made herself obedient with him,
even in his sacrifice. This is why God raised
her above every other creature, and why
Christ crowned Mary the Queen of heaven
and earth.

—BENEDICT XVI
Angelus
November 27, 2006

To Mary, who is the Mother of Mercy and powerful by grace, let loving cries go up from every corner of the earth. From noble temples and the tiniest chapels; from royal palaces and mansions of the rich as from the poorest hut; from war-torn bloody plains and seas, let prayers be heard. Let the anguished cry of mothers and wives, the wailing of innocent little ones, the sighs of every generous heart, come to her. And may Mary's most tender love be moved to gain the peace we seek for our troubled world.

—BENEDICT XV
Letter
May 5, 1917

From the earliest days of the Church, in both victory and crisis, Christians have addressed prayers of petition and hymns of praise and honor to Mary, the Queen of Heaven. The hope they placed in the Mother of the Divine King, Jesus Christ, has never wavered. Neither has our faith in her failed. For Mary rules over the whole world with a mother's goodness even though she is crowned in heaven with the glory of a queen.

—PIUS XII
Ad Caeli Reginam, 1
October 11, 1954

Let all Christians find joy in being subjects of the Virgin Mother of God. For while Mary holds royal power, she is on fire with a mother's love.

. . . Let her churches be filled by the faithful, her feast days honored, and may the beads of the rosary be in the hands of all. May Christians gather in small numbers and large, to sing her praises in churches, in homes, in hospitals, in prisons. May Mary's name be held in highest respect, for it is sweeter than honey and more precious than jewels.

—Pius XII
Ad Caeli Reginam, 43, 48
October 11, 1954

$\mathcal{S}$trengthened by the presence of Christ, the Church journeys through time toward the end of the ages and she goes to meet the Lord when he comes.

But on this journey—and I want to make this point clearly—the Church walks along the path already traveled by the Virgin Mary. . . .

—JOHN PAUL II
Redemptoris Mater, 2
March 25, 1987

Our Lady

help us to trust in human goodness
and in the Father's love
teach us to build up the world
beginning from within:
in the depths of silence and prayer,
in the joy of friendship and love,
and in the rare richness of the cross

H ail Mary, woman of faith, and first of
the disciples!
Virgin Mother of the Church,
help us always to know the source of the
hope that is in us.
Help us trust in human goodness and in the
Father's love.
Teach us to build up the world beginning
from within:
in the depths of silence and prayer,
in the joy of friendship and love,
and in the rare richness of the cross.

Holy Mary, Mother of believers,
Our Lady of Lourdes,
pray for us.
Amen.

—JOHN PAUL II
Prayer to Our Lady of Lourdes
August 15, 2004

$\mathcal{M}$other of all men and women,
I come to you as a son visiting his mother.

. . . As the Successor of Peter,
I wish to present to your Immaculate Heart
the joys and hopes, as well as the problems
    and sufferings
of each one of these sons and daughters
    of yours
who are gathered here, or who are praying
    with us from afar.

Mother most gentle,
you know each one by name.
You know each one's face and life story.
You love them all with a mother's kindness
that wells up from the heart of God's love.

—BENEDICT XVI
At the Shine of Our Lady of Fatima, Portugal
May 12, 2010

Finally, we turn to you, O Blessed Virgin Mary, Mother of Jesus and our Mother also. How can we hope to work on the greatest problem of life or death which overshadows all people, without depending on your prayers to keep us safe from danger? This is your hour, Mary. Jesus entrusted us to you in the final moment of his sacrifice on the cross. We are confident in your help.

—JOHN XXIII
Message for Peace
September 10, 1961

On September 8th, the Holy Church keeps the feast of your most happy birthday. We greet your birth as the first beginning of the world's salvation and the growth of peace. This is what we ask of you, most loving Mother and Queen of the whole world. The world does not need victorious wars and defeated peoples, but new strength of salvation and the calm of peace. This is what it needs, and this is what it cries out for: "the dawn of salvation and the growth of peace. Amen."

—JOHN XXIII
Message for Peace
September 10, 1961

Blessed Mary,
Pope John Paul II visited you in Fatima
    three times.
He thanked the "unseen hand"
that rescued him from death in 1981
when an assassin attempted to kill him
on your feast day, May 13th, in St. Peter's
    Square.

Pope John Paul offered a bullet which
gravely wounded him
to the Shrine of Fatima;
and it was set in the crown of the statue of
    the Queen of Peace.

Mary, it is a deep comfort
to know that you are crowned
not only with the silver and gold of our joys
    and hopes,
but also with the "bullet"
of our worries and sufferings.

—BENEDICT XVI
At the Shine of Our Lady of Fatima, Portugal
May 12, 2010

Our Lady of Jasna Gora, the Bright
    Mountain,
Mother of the Church! Once more I give
    myself completely to you
in your mother's bond of love.
"*Totus tuus!*"—I am all yours!

I consecrate to you the whole Church,
everywhere and to the ends of the earth.
I give to you all humanity;
I give you all men and women, my brothers
    and sisters,
all peoples and all nations.
I give you Europe and all the continents.
I give you Rome and Poland, now united
through your servant by a fresh bond of
    love.

Mother, accept us!
Mother, do not abandon us!
Mother, be our guide!

—JOHN PAUL II
Visit to Our Lady of Czestochowa
June 6, 1979

Loreto Litany
of the
Blessed Virgin Mary

Lord, have mercy on us.
> Christ have mercy on us.

Lord, have mercy on us. Christ, hear us.
> *Christ graciously hear us.*

God, the Father of heaven, *have mercy on us.*

God the Son, Redeemer of the world, *have mercy on us.*

God the Holy Ghost, *have mercy on us.*

Holy Trinity, one God, *have mercy on us.*

Holy Mary, *pray for us.*

Holy Mother of God,

Holy Virgin of virgins,

Mother of Christ,

Mother of the Church,
> *(added by John Paul II in 1980)*

Mother of divine grace,

Mother most pure,

Mother most chaste,

Mother inviolate,

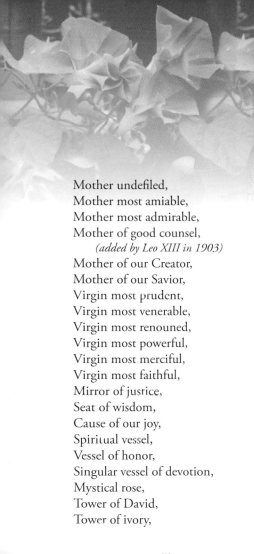

Mother undefiled,
Mother most amiable,
Mother most admirable,
Mother of good counsel,
   (added by Leo XIII in 1903)
Mother of our Creator,
Mother of our Savior,
Virgin most prudent,
Virgin most venerable,
Virgin most renouned,
Virgin most powerful,
Virgin most merciful,
Virgin most faithful,
Mirror of justice,
Seat of wisdom,
Cause of our joy,
Spiritual vessel,
Vessel of honor,
Singular vessel of devotion,
Mystical rose,
Tower of David,
Tower of ivory,

House of gold,
Ark of the covenant,
Gate of heaven,
Morning star,
Health of the sick,
Refuge of sinners,
Comforter of the afflicted,
Help of Christians,
Queen of Angels,
Queen of Patriarchs,
Queen of Prophets,
Queen of Apostles,
Queen of Martyrs,
Queen of Confessors,
Queen of Virgins,
Queen of all Saints,
Queen conceived without original sin,
   (added by Leo XIII in 1883)
Queen assumed into heaven,
   (added by Pius XII in 1950)
Queen of the most holy Rosary,
   (added by Clement X in 1675)
Queen of families,
   (added by John Paul II in 1995)
Queen of Peace,
   (added by Benedict XV in 1917)

Lamb of God, you take away the sins of the world,
spare us, O Lord.

Lamb of God, you take away the sins of the world,
graciously hear us, O Lord.

Lamb of God, you take away the sins of the world,
have mercy on us.

Pray for us, O holy Mother of God.
That we may be made worthy of the promises of Christ.

Let us pray. Grant, we beseech thee, O Lord God, unto us thy servants, that we may rejoice in continual health of mind and body; and, by the glorious intercession of Blessed Mary ever Virgin, may be delivered from present sadness, and enter into the joy of thine eternal gladness. Through Christ our Lord. *Amen.*

—Approved by Sixtus V,
in 1587

Meet
the Popes
You've
Prayed
With

Holy Father

Our Popes

Supreme Pontiff

Benedict XVI

Elected our 265th pope
on April 19, 2005

Joseph Ratzinger was born—and baptized—on Holy
Saturday, April 16, 1927. His father was a policeman.
The youngest of three children, Joseph grew up in
Bavaria, Germany during very difficult times. His
family opposed Hitler and believed that Nazism was
against their Catholic faith. At the end of the war,

Patriarch of the West

Servant of the Servants of God

Shepherd of the Universal Church

Bishop of Rome

Joseph and his brother entered the seminary. They were ordained on the same day in 1951. A brilliant theologian, Fr. Ratzinger was a professor for many years. He was appointed Archbishop of Munich and Freiberg in 1977, and cardinal a few months later. From 1981–2005, Cardinal Ratzinger served as the head of the Church's Congregation for the Doctrine of the Faith. Elected Pope in 2005, he chose the name Benedict.

Blessed John Paul II

Served as our 264th pope from
October 16, 1978–April 2, 2005

Karol Josef Wojtyla was born May 18, 1920 in
southern Poland. By the age of twenty, Karol had
lost all the members of his immediate family. During
World War II, he was an actor and playwright,
learned many languages, worked in a factory, and
studied secretly for the priesthood. Ordained in
1946, he was named Bishop of Krakow in 1958,
appointed archbishop in 1964, and cardinal in 1967.
Cardinal Wojtyla was elected Pope in 1978, the first
non-Italian in 455 years. He was shot by a terrorist
on May 13, 1981. John Paul later thanked Our
Lady of Fatima for his survival. One of the bullets
that struck him was set in the crown of her statue in
Portugal. During his twenty-six years as Pope, John
Paul II worked to defeat communism, traveled to 129
countries, added five new mysteries to the Rosary,
and canonized over 480 new saints. He died in 2005,
and was beatified on May 1, 2011.

Servant of God Paul VI

Served as our 262nd pope from
June 21, 1963–August 6, 1978

Giovanni Battista Enrico Antonio Maria Montini
was born September 26, 1897 in Concesio, Italy.

Giovanni's education was often interrupted by illness. He was ordained in 1920. After a short time in Poland, Fr. Montini became a university chaplain, and encouraged students to stand against the dictator Mussolini. Close to Pius XII, Fr. Montini was appointed Bishop of Milan in 1954. He was appointed a cardinal in 1958, and elected Pope in 1963. Paul VI was the last pope to be crowned in a royal ceremony. He completed Vatican II, was the first pope to visit Africa, and the first to travel to five continents. He sent a goodwill message left on the moon by Apollo 11 astronauts. Paul VI died in 1978.

Blessed John XXIII

Served as our 261st pope from October 28, 1958–June 3, 1963

Angelo Giuseppe Roncalli was born on November 25, 1881 in a small Italian village. His family worked as tenant farmers. Angelo was ordained in 1904. Fr. Roncalli was drafted into the Italian army during World War I, and served in the medical corps and as a chaplain. He was named a bishop in 1925, and used his position to help Jewish refugees. In 1953, Bishop Roncalli was appointed Patriarch of Venice and made a cardinal. He was elected Pope in 1958, and was the first to choose the name "John" in over 500 years. John XXIII called the Second Vatican Council, but died in 1963 before its conclusion. He was beatified in 2000.

Venerable Pius XII

Served as our 260th pope from
March 2, 1939–October 9, 1958

Eugenio Maria Giuseppe Giovanni Pacelli was born
March 2, 1876 in Rome. By the time he was twelve,
Eugenio had expressed interest in becoming a priest.
He was ordained on Easter Sunday in 1899. Fr.
Pacelli turned down offers to teach canon law in
Rome and at The Catholic University of America,
and served as a Vatican diplomat instead. He became
a bishop in 1917, a cardinal in 1929, and was then
appointed Vatican Secretary of State. Cardinal Pacelli
was elected Pope in 1939 on his sixty-third birthday.
He guided the Church during World War II, restored
the Easter Vigil liturgy, and emphasized the Bible. In
1950, Pius XII proclaimed the Church's belief in the
Assumption of Mary. He died in 1958.

Pius XI

Served as our 259th pope from
February 6, 1922–February 10, 1939

Ambrogio Damiano Achille Ratti was born on May
31, 1857 near Milan, which was then part of the
Austrian Empire. His father was a silk manufacturer.
He was ordained in 1879. Fr. Ratti was a mountain
climber and librarian, and was known as a scholar of

ancient writing. He worked in the Vatican Library, and later as a Church diplomat. Fr. Ratti was made a bishop in 1919 and named Cardinal Archbishop of Milan in 1921. He was elected Pope in 1922. Pius XI tried to secure the freedom of the Church and condemned Nazi racism. He established the feast of Christ the King. Pius XI died in 1939, just before the beginning of World War II.

Benedict XV

Served as our 258th pope from
September 3, 1914–January 22, 1922

Giacomo Paolo Giovanni Battista della Chiesa was born November 21, 1854 near Genoa, Italy. His father rejected his desire for priesthood, and insisted that he become a lawyer. After Giacomo finished his law degree, he asked to become a priest again. He was ordained in 1878. Fr. Della Chiesa served as a diplomat until he was named Archbishop of Bologna in 1907. He was made a cardinal in May of 1914, and elected Pope just three months later. Benedict XV focused on World War I. He worked tirelessly for peace, but without much success. Placing the whole world under Mary's protection, he added "Queen of Peace" to the Litany of the Blessed Virgin. Benedict XV died in 1922.

Saint Pius X

Served as our 257th pope from
August 4, 1903–August 20, 1914

The second of ten children, Giuseppe Melchiorre
Sarto was born on June 2, 1835, in Riese, a village
then part of the Austrian Empire. His family was
poor, but he was given a scholarship to the Seminary
of Padua, and ordained a priest in 1858. Fr. Sarto
became Bishop of Treviso in 1879, then cardinal—
and the Patriarch of Venice—in1893. He was elected
Pope in 1903. Known as the *Pope of the Blessed
Sacrament*, Pius X promoted daily communion, and
reduced the age of First Communion from fourteen
to seven. He died shortly after the outbreak of World
War I. Canonized in 1954, Pius X is the most recent
Pope to have been made a saint.

Leo XIII, OFS

Served as our 256th pope from
February 20, 1878–July 20, 1903

Vincenzo Gioacchino Raffaele Luigi Pecci was
born near Rome on March 2, 1810. The sixth of
seven sons, Vincenzo had a gifted mind. He wrote
poems in Latin at the age of eleven and won many

academic awards. Ordained in 1837, Fr. Pecci served as ambassador to Belgium, and later as Archbishop of Perugia. Elected Pope in 1878, Leo XIII reached out to the modern world with special concern for family life and social justice. Known for promoting the Rosary, Leo XIII is called the *Rosary Pope*. Leo XIII was the first pope to make a voice recording and appear on film. Living to the age of ninety-three, Leo XIII was the oldest pope.

Blessed Pius IX, OFS

Served as our 256th pope from June 16, 1846 until February 20, 1878

Giovanni Maria Mastai-Ferretti was born into a noble family on May 13, 1792. He was ordained in 1819. Fr. Mastai-Ferretti suffered from a form of epilepsy, but his illness improved as he grew older. He spent two years assisting Church finances in Chile. Returning to Italy at thirty-five, he was appointed Archbishop of Spoleto and named a cardinal in 1839. He was elected Pope in 1846. Pope for more than thirty-one years, Pius IX was the longest serving pope in history. Strongly devoted to Mary, he proclaimed the dogma of the Immaculate Conception. He called the First Vatican Council, wrote a record thirty-eight encyclicals, and was the first pope to be photographed. Pius IX died in 1878, and was beatified by John Paul II in 2000.

Sixtus V, OFM Conv.

Served as our 227th pope from
April 24, 1585 until August 27, 1590

Felice Peretti was born to a poor family on December
13, 1521. Felice was a swineherd until he became a
Franciscan novice at the age of twelve. Ordained in
1547, Fr. Peretti quickly gained a reputation as an
excellent preacher. He was invited to preach Lenten
sermons in Rome. There he met the leading cardinals
of his day, as well as future saints Philip Neri and
Ignatius. Pius V appointed him bishop, and later
cardinal. Bishop Peretti was also the Pope's confessor.
During the reign of Gregory XIII, Cardinal Peretti
collected art and edited the works of St. Ambrose.
Elected Pope in 1585, Sixtus V rebuilt Church
finances, reformed Church government, rid Rome
of thousands of bandits, and approved the Loreto
Litany of the Blessed Virgin Mary, which is still
prayed today. He died in 1590.

Photo credits:

Pauline
BOOKS & MEDIA

The Daughters of St. Paul operate book and media centers at the following addresses. Visit, call or write the one nearest you today, or find us on the World Wide Web, www.pauline.org

CALIFORNIA
3908 Sepulveda Blvd, Culver City, CA 90230   310-397-8676
935 Brewster Avenue, Redwood City, CA 94063   650-369-4230
5945 Balboa Avenue, San Diego, CA 92111   858-565-9181

FLORIDA
145 S.W. 107th Avenue, Miami, FL 33174   305-559-6715

HAWAII
1143 Bishop Street, Honolulu, HI 96813   808-521-2731
Neighbor Islands call: 866-521-2731

ILLINOIS
172 North Michigan Avenue, Chicago, IL 60601   312-346-4228

LOUISIANA
4403 Veterans Memorial Blvd, Metairie, LA 70006   504-887-7631

MASSACHUSETTS
885 Providence Hwy, Dedham, MA 02026   781-326-5385

MISSOURI
9804 Watson Road, St. Louis, MO 63126   314-965-3512

NEW YORK
64 West 38th Street, New York, NY 10018   212-754-1110

PENNSYLVANIA
Philadelphia—relocating   215-969-5068

SOUTH CAROLINA
243 King Street, Charleston, SC 29401   843-577-0175

VIRGINIA
1025 King Street, Alexandria, VA 22314   703-549-3806

CANADA
3022 Dufferin Street, Toronto, ON M6B 3T5   416-781-9131